Spiritual Progress
and
Practical Occultism

By Helena P. Blavatsky

Copyright © 2021 Lamp of Trismegistus. All rights reserved. No part of this publication may be reproduced or transmitted in any form or by any means, electronic or mechanical, including photocopying, recording, or by any information storage and retrieval system, without permission in writing from Lamp of Trismegistus. Reviewers may quote brief passages.

ISBN: 978-1-63118-583-0

Esoteric Classics

Other Books in this Series and Related Titles

Aurora of the Philosophers by Paracelsus (978-1-63118-507-6)

Clairvoyance and Psychic Abilities by A Besant &c (978-1-63118-403-1)

The Feminine Occult by various authors (978-1-63118-711-7)

Rosicrucian Rules, Secret Signs, Codes and Symbols by various (978-1-63118-488-8)

An Outline of Theosophy by C W Leadbeater (978-1-63118-452-9)

Paracelsus, the Four Elements and Their Spirits by M P Hall (978-1-63118-400-0)

Essays on Ancient Magic by Helena P Blavatsky (978-1-63118-535-9)

Essays on the Esoteric Tradition of Karma by A Besant &c (978-1-63118-426-0)

The Use of Evil by Annie Besant (978-1-63118-532-8)

Occult Arts by William Q. Judge (978-1-63118-559-5)

The Alchemical Catechism of Paracelsus by Paracelsus (978-1-63118-513-7)

Alchemy in the Nineteenth Century by Helena P Blavatsky (978-1-63118-446-8)

Qabbalistic Teachings and the Tree of Life by M P Hall (978-1-63118-482-6)

The Historic, Mythic and Mystic Christ by Annie Besant (978–1–63118–533–5)

The Hidden Mysteries of Christianity by Annie Besant (978–1–63118–534–2)

History, Analysis and Secret Tradition of the Tarot by Hall &c (978-1-63118-445-1)

Kali the Mother by Sister Nivedita (978-1-63118-558-8)

Arcane Formulas or Mental Alchemy by W W Atkinson (978-1-63118-459-8)

The Machinery of the Mind by Dion Fortune (978-1-63118-451-2)

Vision of the Spirit by C. Jinarajadasa (978-1-63118-560-1)

The Leadbeater Reader: A Selection of Occult Essays (978-1-63118-483-3)

Audio versions are also available on Audible, Amazon and Apple

Other Books in this Series and Related Titles

Memory and Consciousness by Besant & Blavatsky (978–1–63118–582–3)

The Origin of Evil by Helena P Blavatsky (978–1–63118–581–6)

The Camp of Philosophy: Studies in Alchemy by Bloomfield (978–1–63118–580–9)

The Testaments of the Twelve Patriarchs (978–1–63118–579–3)

Occult or Exact Science? by Helena P Blavatsky (978–1–63118–578–6)

Occultism, Semi-Occultism & Pseudo Occultism by A Besant (978–1–63118–577–9)

The Fourth-Gospel and Synoptical Problem by G R S Mead (978–1–63118–576–2)

On the Bhagavad-Gita by T Subba Row &c (978–1–63118–575–5)

What Theosophy Does for Us by C W Leadbeater (978–1–63118–574–8)

Spiritual Life for Man by Annie Besant (978–1–63118–573–1)

The Mysteries by Annie Besant (978–1–63118–572–4)

Fundamental Ideas of Theosophy by Bhagwan Das (978–1–63118–571–7)

Dreams: What They Are and Caused by C W Leadbeater (978–1–63118–570–0)

Communication Between Different Worlds by Annie Besant (978–1–63118–569–4)

Animism, Magic and the Omnipotence of Thought by S Freud (978–1–63118–568–7)

Buddhism by F Otto Schrader (978–1–63118–567–0)

Death by W W Westcott (978–1–63118–566–3)

The Religion of Theosophy by Bhagwan Das (978–1–63118–565–6)

The Spirit of Zoroastrianism by Henry S Olcott (978–1–63118–564–9)

The Brotherhood of Religions by Annie Besant (978–1–63118–563–2)

Fourth Book of Maccabees by Josephus (978-1-63118-562-5)

Audio versions are also available on Audible, Amazon and Apple

Table of Contents

Introduction...7

Spiritual Progress...9

Practical Occultism...17

Spiritualism and Occult Truth...27

Occultism Versus the Occult Arts...37

Occultism is not the acquirement of powers, whether psychic or intellectual, though both are its servants. Neither is occultism the pursuit of happiness, as men understand the word; for the first step is sacrifice, the second, renunciation. Occultism is the science of life, the art of living.

INTRODUCTION

The word "esoteric" can be difficult to define. Esotericism in general can be seen less as a system of beliefs and more as a category, which encompasses numerous, different systems of beliefs. It's a bit of juxtaposition, since the word "esoteric" indicates something that few people know about, while the term itself broadly covers numerous philosophies, practices, areas of study and belief systems.

In a greater sense, Esotericism acts as a storehouse for secret knowledge, which is often considered ancient (by *tradition, if not by fact),* passed down from generation to generation, in private. At various times in history, simply possessing the knowledge of some of these subjects, was considered illegal and a jailable offence, if discovered. This usually included such general topics as Alchemy, Pharmacology, Qabalah, Hermeticism, Occultism, Ceremonial Magic, Astrology, Divination, Rosicrucianism and so on. Collectively, these areas of study were often referred to as the esoteric sciences.

Sometimes, the outer garment of a subject isn't esoteric, while what is hidden beneath it, is. As an example, Freemasonry isn't necessarily esoteric by nature (at *least not anymore),* but certain signs, passwords and handshakes given to the candidate during their initiation, are in fact, esoteric, in the sense that they are hidden from the general public.

Today, in the twenty-first century, such topics are readily available at bookstores across the country, and numerous mainsteam publishers offer beginners guides and coffee-table volumes on many of these subjects, intended for mass appeal. Books like *"The Secret"* have turned previously arcane topics into household knowledge. All that being the case, however, it isn't to say that there still aren't buried secrets to uncover, ancient wisdom being ignored and forgotten mysteries to be explored. In fact, it is often that we are only able to further our own studies by standing on the shoulders of these disappearing giants.

Lamp of Trismegistus is doing its part to help preserve humanity's esoteric history by making some of these classics available to those students who are seeking to unearth the knowledge of these ancient colossi.

So, be sure to check other titles from our *Esoteric Classics* series, as well as our *Occult Fiction*, *Theosophical Classics*, *Foundations of Freemasonry Series*, *Supernatural Fiction*, *Paranormal Research Series*, *Studies in Buddhism* and our *Christian Apocrypha Series*. You can also download the audio versions of most of these titles from Amazon, Apple or Audible, for learning on the go.

SPIRITUAL PROGRESS

CHRISTINA ROSSETTI's well-known lines:

Does the road wind up-hill all the way? Yes, to the very end.
Does the journey take the whole long day? From morn to night, my friend.

are like an epitome of the life of those who are truly treading the path which leads to higher things. Whatever differences are to be found in the various presentations of the Esoteric Doctrine, as in every age it donned a fresh garment, different both in hue and texture to that which preceded; yet in every one of them we find the fullest agreement upon one point -- the road to spiritual development. One only inflexible rule has been ever binding upon the neophyte, as it is binding now -- the *complete* subjugation of the lower nature by the higher. From the Vedas and Upanishads (Upanishats) to the recently published *Light on the Path,* search as we may through the bibles of every race and cult, we find but one only way, -- hard, painful, troublesome, by which men can gain the true spiritual insight. And how can it be otherwise, since all religions and all philosophies are but the variants of the first teachings of the One Wisdom, imparted to men at the beginning of the cycle by the Planetary Spirit?

The true Adept, the developed man, must, we are always told, *become* -- he cannot be made. The process is therefore one of growth through evolution, and this must necessarily involve a certain amount of pain.

The main cause of pain lies in our perpetually seeking the permanent in the impermanent, and not only seeking, but acting as if we had already found the unchangeable in a world of which the one certain quality we can predicate is constant change; and always, just as we fancy we have taken a firm hold upon the permanent, it changes within our very grasp, and pain results.

Again, the idea of growth involves also the idea of disruption: the inner being must continually burst through its confining shell or encasement, and such a disruption must also be accompanied by pain, not physical but mental and intellectual.

And this is how it is, in the course of our lives, the trouble that comes upon us is always just the one we feel to be the hardest that could possibly happen -- it is always the one thing we feel we cannot possibly bear. If we look at it from a wider point of view, we shall see that we are trying to burst through our shell at its one vulnerable point; that our growth, to be real growth, and not the collective result of a series of excrescence, must progress evenly throughout, just as the body of a child grows, not first the head and then a hand, followed perhaps by a leg, but in all directions at once, regularly and imperceptibly. Man's tendency is to cultivate each part separately, neglecting the others in the meantime -- every crushing pain is caused by the expansion of some neglected part, which expansion is rendered more difficult by the effects of the cultivation bestowed elsewhere.

Evil is often the result of over-anxiety, and men are always trying to do too much, they are not content to leave well alone, to do always just what the occasion demands and no more; they exaggerate every action and so produce karma to be worked out in a future birth.

One of the subtlest forms of this evil is the hope and desire of reward. Many there are who, albeit often unconsciously, are yet spoiling all their efforts by entertaining this idea of reward, and allowing it to become an active factor in their lives, and so leaving the door open to anxiety, doubt, fear, despondency — failure.

The goal of the aspirant for spiritual wisdom is entrance upon a higher plane of existence; he is to become a new man, more perfect in every way than he is at present, and if he succeeds, his capabilities and faculties will receive a corresponding increase of range and power, just as in the visible world we find that each stage in the evolutionary scale is marked by increase of capacity.

This is how it is that the Adept becomes endowed with marvellous powers that have been so often described, but the main point to be remembered is, that these powers are the natural accompaniments of existence on a higher plane of evolution, just as the ordinary human faculties are the natural accompaniments of existence on the ordinary human plane.

Many persons seem to think that adeptship is not so much the result of radical development as of additional construction; they seem to imagine that an Adept is a man, who, by going through a certain plainly defined course of training, consisting of minute attention to a set of arbitrary rules, acquires first one power and then another; and, when he has attained a certain number of these powers is forthwith dubbed an adept. Acting on this mistaken idea, they fancy that the first thing to be done towards attaining adeptship is to acquire "powers" — clairvoyance and the power of leaving the physical body and travelling to a distance are among those which fascinate the most.

To those who wish to acquire such powers for their own private advantage, we have nothing to say; they fall under the condemnation of all who act for purely selfish ends. But there are others, who, mistaking effect for cause, honestly think that the acquirement of abnormal powers is the only road to spiritual advancement. These look upon our Society as merely the readiest means to enable them to gain knowledge in this direction, considering it as a sort of occult academy, an institution established to afford facilities for the instruction of would-be miracle-workers. In spite of repeated protests and warnings, there are some minds in whom this notion seems ineradicably fixed, and they are loud in their expressions of disappointment when they find that what had been previously told them is perfectly true; that the Society was founded to teach no new and easy paths to the acquisition of "powers"; and that its only mission is to rekindle the torch of truth, so long extinguished for all but the very few, and to keep that truth alive by the formation of a fraternal union of mankind, the only soil in which the good seed can grow. The Theosophical Society does indeed desire to promote the spiritual growth of every individual who comes within its influence, but its methods are those of the ancient Rishis (Rshis), its tenets those of the oldest Esotericism; it is no dispenser of patent nostrums composed of violent remedies which no honest dealer would dare to use.

In this connection we would warn all our members, and others who are seeking spiritual knowledge, to beware of persons offering to teach them easy methods of acquiring psychic gifts; such gifts *(laukika)* are indeed comparatively easy of acquirement by artificial means, but fade out as soon as the nerve-stimulus exhausts itself. The real seership and Adeptship which is accompanied by true psychic development *(lokothra) (sometimes lokottara)*, once reached, is never lost.

It appears that various societies have sprung into existence since the foundation of the Theosophical Society, profiting by the interest the latter has awakened in matters of psychic research, and endeavouring to gain members by promising them easy acquirement of psychic powers. In India we have long been familiar with the existence of hosts of sham ascetics of all descriptions, and we fear that there is fresh danger in this direction, here, as well as in Europe and America. We only hope that none of our members, dazzled by brilliant promises, will allow themselves to be taken in by self-deluded dreamers, or, it may be, wilful deceivers.

To show that some real necessity exists for our protests and warnings, we may mention that we have recently seen, enclosed in a letter from Benares, copies of an advertisement put forth by a so-called "Mahatma." He calls for "eight men and women who know English and any of the Indian vernaculars well"; and concludes by saying that "those who want to know particulars of the work and *the amount of pay*" should apply to his address, with enclosed postage stamps! Upon the table before us lies a reprint of "The Divine Pymander", published in England last year, and which contains a notice to "*Theosophists who may have been disappointed in their expectations of Sublime Wisdom being freely dispensed by* HINDOO MAHATMAS"; cordially inviting them to send in their names to the Editor, who will see them, "after a short probation", admitted into an Occult Brotherhood who "teach *freely* and WITHOUT RESERVE all they find worthy to receive". Strangely enough, we find in the very volume in question Hermes Trismegistus saying:

"For this only, O Son, is the way to *Truth,* which our progenitors traveled in; and by which making their journey, they a length attained to the good. It is a venerable way and plain, but hard and difficult for the soul to go in that is in the body.

"Werefore we must look warily to such kind of people, that being in ignorance they may be less evil for fear of that which is hidden and secret."

It is perfectly true that some Theosophists have been (through nobody's fault but their own) greatly disappointed because we have offered them no short cut to Yoga Vidya, and there are others who wish for practical work. And, significantly enough, those who have done least for the Society are loudest in fault-finding. Now, why do not these persons and all our members who are able to do so, take up the serious study of mesmerism? Mesmerism has been called the Key to the Occult Sciences, and it has this advantage that it offers peculiar opportunities for doing good to mankind. If in each of our branches we were able to establish a homeopathic dispensary with the addition of mesmeric healing, such as has already been done with great success in Bombay, we might contribute towards putting the science of medicine in this country on a sounder basis, and be the means of incalculable benefit to the people at large.

There are others of our branches, besides the one at Bombay, that have done good work in this direction, but there is room for infinitely more to be done than has yet been attempted. And the same is the case in the various other departments of the Society's work. It would be a good thing if the members of each branch would put their heads together and seriously consult as to what tangible steps they can take to further the declared objects of the Society. In too many cases the members of the Theosophical Society content themselves with a somewhat superficial study of its books, without making any real contribution to its active work. If the Society is to be a power for good in this and other lands, it can only bring about this result by the active cooperation of every one of its members, and we would earnestly appeal to each of them to consider carefully what possibilities of work are within his power, and then to *earnestly set about carrying them into effect.* Right thought is a good thing, but thought alone does not count for much unless it is translated into action. There is not a single member in the Society who is not able to do *something* to aid the cause of truth and universal brotherhood; it only depends on his own will, to make that *something* an accomplished fact.

Above all we would reiterate the fact that the Society is no nursery for incipient Adepts; teachers cannot be provided to go round and give instruction to various branches on the different subjects which come within the Society's work of investigation; the Branches must study for themselves; books are to be had, and the knowledge there put forth must be practically applied by the various members: thus will be developed self-reliance and reasoning powers. We urge this strongly; for appeals have reached us that any lecturer sent to Branches must be practically versed in experimental psychology and clairvoyance *(i.e.,* looking into magic mirrors and reading the future, etc., etc.). Now we consider that such experiments should originate amongst members themselves to be of any value in the development of the individual or to enable him to make progress in his "uphill" path, and therefore earnestly recommend our members to *try* for them .

PRACTICAL OCCULTISM

There are many people who are looking for practical instruction in Occultism. It becomes necessary, therefore, to state once for all;

(a) The essential difference between theoretical and practical Occultism; or what is generally known as Theosophy on the one hand, and Occult science on the other, and:

(b) The nature of the difficulties involved in the study of the latter.

It is easy to become a Theosophist. Any person of average intellectual capacities, and a leaning toward the metaphysical; of pure, unselfish life, who finds more joy in helping his neighbour than in receiving help himself; one who is every ready to sacrifice his own pleasures for the sake of other people; and who loves Truth, Goodness and Wisdom for their own sake, not for the benefit they may confer — is a Theosophist.

But it is quite another matter to put oneself upon the path which leads to the knowledge of what is good to do, as to the right discrimination of good from evil; a path which also leads a man to that power through which he can do the good he desires, often without even apparently lifting a finger.

Moreover, there is one important fact with which the student should be made acquainted. Namely, the enormous, almost limitless, responsibility assumed by the teacher for the sake of the pupil. From the Gurus of the East who teach openly or secretly, down to the few Kabalists in Western lands who undertake to teach the rudiments of the Sacred Science to their disciples — those Western Hierophants being often themselves ignorant of the danger they incur — one and all of those "Teachers" are subject to the same inviolable law. From the moment they begin *really* to teach, from the instant they confer *any* power — whether psychic, mental or physical — on their pupils, they take upon themselves *all* the sins of that pupil, in connection with the Occult Sciences, whether of omission or commission, until the moment when initiation makes the pupil a Master and responsible in his turn. There is a weird and mystic religious law, greatly reverenced and acted upon in the Greek, half-forgotten in the Roman Catholic, and absolutely extinct in the Protestant Church. It dates from the earliest days of Christianity, and has its basis in the law just stated, of which it was a symbol and an expression. This is the dogma of the absolute sacredness of the relation between the god-parents who stand sponsors for a child [So holy is the connection thus formed deemed in the Greek Church, that a marriage between god-parents of the same child is regarded as the worst kind of incest, is considered illegal and is dissolved by law; and this absolute prohibition extends even to the children of one of the sponsors as regards those of the other] These tacitly take upon themselves all the sins of the newly baptized child — (anointed as at the initiation, a mystery truly!) — until the day when the child becomes a responsible unit, knowing good and evil. Thus it is clear why the "Teachers" are so reticent, and why "Chelas" are required to serve a seven years' probation to prove their fitness, and develop the qualities necessary to the security of both Master and pupil.

Occultism is not magic. It is *comparatively* easy to learn the trick of spells and the methods of using the subtler, but still material, forces of physical nature; the powers of the animal soul in man are soon awakened; the forces which his love, his hate, his passion, can call into operation, are readily developed. But this is Black Magic — *Sorcery*. For it is the motive, and *the motive alone*, which makes any exercise of power become black, malignant, or white, beneficent Magic. It is impossible to employ *spiritual* forces if there is the slightest tinge of selfishness remaining in the operator. For, unless the intention is entirely unalloyed, the spiritual will transform itself into the psychic, act on the astral plane, and dire results may be produced by it. The powers and forces of animal nature can equally be used by the selfish and revengeful, as by the unselfish and the all-forgiving; the powers and forces of spirit lend themselves only to the perfectly pure in heart — and this is DIVINE MAGIC.

What are then the conditions required to become a student of the "Divina Sapientia"? For let it be know that no such instruction can possibly be given unless these certain conditions are complied with, and rigorously carried out during the years of study. This is a *sine qua non*. No man can swim unless he enters deep water. No bird can fly unless its wings are grown, and it has space before it and courage to trust itself to the air. A man who will wield a two-edged sword, must be a thorough master of the blunt weapon, if he would not injure himself — or what is worse — others, at the first attempt.

To give an approximate idea of the conditions under which alone the study of Divine Wisdom can be pursued with safety, that is, without danger that Divine will give place to Black Magic, a page is given from the "private rules", with which every instructor in the East is furnished. The few passages which follow are chosen from a great number and explained in brackets.

1— The place selected for receiving instruction must be a spot calculated not to distract the mind, and filled with "influence-evolving" (magnetic) objects. The five sacred colours gathered in a circle must be there among other things. The place must be free from any malignant influences hanging about in the air.

[The place must be set apart, and used for no other purpose. The five "sacred colours" are the prismatic hues arranged in a certain way, as these colours are very magnetic. By "malignant influences" are meant any disturbances through strifes, quarrels, bad feelings, *etc.*, as these are said to impress themselves immediately on the astral light, *i.e.*, in the atmosphere of the place, and to hang "about in the air". This first condition seems easy enough to accomplish, yet — on further consideration, it is one of the most difficult ones to obtain.]

2— Before the disciple shall be permitted to study "face to face", he has to acquire preliminary understanding in a select company of other lay *upasaka* (disciples), the number of whom must be odd.

["Face to face", means in this instance a study independent or apart from others, when the disciple gets his instruction *face to face* either with himself (his higher, Divine Self) or — his guru. It is then only that each receives *his due* of information, according to the use he has made of his knowledge. This can happen only toward the end of the cycle of instruction.]

3— Before thou (the teacher) shall impart to thy *Lanoo* (disciple) the good (holy) words of LAMRIN or shall permit him "to make ready" for *Dubjed*, thou shalt take care that his mind is thoroughly purified and at peace with all, especially with *his other Selves*. Otherwise the words of Wisdom and of the good Law shall scatter and be picked up by the winds.

["Lamrin" is a work of practical instructions, by Tson-kha-pa, in two portions, one for ecclesiastical and exoteric purposes, the other for esoteric use. "To make ready" for *Dubjed*, is to prepare the vessels used for seership, such as mirrors and crystals. The "other selves" refers to the fellow-students. Unless the greatest harmony reigns among the learners, *no* success is possible. It is the teacher who makes the selections according to the magnetic and electric natures of the students, bringing together and adjusting most carefully the positive and the negative elements.]

4— The *upasaka* while studying must take care to be united as the fingers on one hand. Thou shalt impress upon their minds that whatever hurts one should hurt the others; and if the rejoicing of one finds no echo in the breasts of the others, then the required conditions are absent, and it is useless to proceed.

[This can hardly happen if the preliminary choice made was consistent with the magnetic requirements. It is known that chelas otherwise promising and fit for the reception of truth, had to wait for years on account of their temper and the impossibility they felt to put themselves *in tune* with their companions. For —]

5— The co-disciples must be tuned by the guru as the strings of a lute (vina), each different from the others, yet each emitting sounds in harmony with all. Collectively they must form a key-board answering in all its parts to thy lightest touch (the touch of the Master). Thus their minds shall open for the harmonies of Wisdom, to vibrate as knowledge through each and all, resulting in effects pleasing to the presiding gods (tutelary or patron-angels) and useful to the Lanoo. So shall Wisdom be impressed for ever on their hearts and the harmony of the law shall never be broken.

6— Those who desire to acquire the knowledge leading to the *Siddhis* (occult powers) have to renounce all the vanities of life and of the world (here follows enumeration of the Siddhis).

7— None can feel the difference between himself and his fellow-students, such as "I am the wisest", "I am more holy and pleasing to the teacher, or in my community, than my brother", etc., — and remain an upasaka. His thoughts must be predominantly fixed upon his heart, chasing therefrom every hostile thought to any living being. It (the heart) must be full of the feeling of its non-separateness from the rest of beings as from all in Nature; otherwise no success can follow.

8— A *Lanoo* (disciple) has to dread external living influence alone (magnetic emanations from living creatures). For this reason, while at one with all, in his *inner nature*, he must take care to separate his outer (external) body from every foreign influence: none must drink out of, or eat in his cup but himself. He must avoid bodily contact *(i.e.,* being touched or touch) with human, as with animal being.

[No pet animals are permitted, and it is forbidden even to touch certain trees and plants. A disciple has to live, so to say, in his own atmosphere in order to individualise it for occult purposes.]

9— The mind must remain blunt to all but the universal truths in nature, lest the "Doctrine of the Heart" should become only the "Doctrine of the Eye" (*i.e.,* empty exoteric ritualism).

10— No animal food of whatever kind, nothing that has life in it, should be taken by the disciple. No wine, no spirits or opium should be used; for these are like the *Lhamayin* (evil spirits), who fasten upon the unwary, they devour the understanding.

[Wine and Spirits are supposed to contain and preserve the bad magnetism of all the men who helped in their fabrication; the meat of each animal, to preserve the psychic characteristics of its kind.]

11— Meditation, abstinence in all, the observation of moral duties, gentle thoughts, good deeds and kind words, as goodwill to all and entire oblivion of Self, are the most efficacious means of obtaining knowledge and preparing for the reception of higher wisdom.

12— It is only by virtue of a strict observance of the foregoing rules that a Lanoo can hope to acquire in good time the Siddhis of the Arhats, the growth which makes him become gradually One with the UNIVERSAL ALL.

These 12 extracts are taken from among some 73 rules, to enumerate which would be useless as they would be meaningless in Europe. But even these few are enough to show the immensity of the difficulties which beset the path of the would-be "Upasaka", who has been born and bred in Western lands. [Be it remembered that *all* "Chelas", even lay disciples, are called Upasaka until after their first initiation, when they become Lanoo-Upasaka. To that day, even those who belong to Lamaseries and are *set apart*, are considered as "laymen"].

All Western, and especially English, education is instinct with the principle of emulation and strife; each boy is urged to learn more quickly, to outstrip his companions, and to surpass them in every possible way. What is mis-called "friendly rivalry" is assiduously cultivated, and the same spirit is fostered and strengthened in every detail of life.

With such ideas "educated into" him from his childhood, how can a Western bring himself to feel towards his co-students "as the fingers on one hand"? Those co-students, too, are not of his *own election*, or chosen by himself from personal sympathy and appreciation. They are chosen by his teacher on far other grounds, and he who would be a student must *first* be strong enough to kill out in his heart all feelings of dislike and antipathy to others. How many Westerns are ready even to attempt this in earnest?

And then the details of daily life, the command not to touch even the hand of one's nearest and dearest. How contrary to Western notions of affection and good feeling! How cold and hard it seems. Egotistical too, people would say, to abstain from giving pleasure to others for the sake of one's own development. Well, let those who think so defer till another lifetime the attempt to enter the path in real earnest. But let them not glory in their own fancied unselfishness. For, in reality, it is only the seeming appearances which they allow to deceive them, the conventional notions, based on emotionalism and gush, or so- called courtesy, things of the unreal life, not the dictates of Truth.

But even putting aside these difficulties, which may be considered "external", though their importance is none the less great, how are students in the West to "attune themselves" to harmony as here required of them? So strong has personality grown in Europe and America, that there is no school of artists even whose members do not hate and are not jealous of each other. "Professional" hatred and envy have become proverbial; men seek each to benefit himself at all costs, and even the so-called courtesies of life are but a hollow mask covering these demons of hatred and jealousy.

In the East the spirit of "non-separateness" is inculcated as steadily from childhood up, as in the West the spirit of rivalry. Personal ambition, personal feelings and desires, are not encouraged to grow so rampant there. When the soil is naturally good, it is cultivated in the right way, and the child grows into a man in whom the habit of subordination of one's lower to one's higher Self is strong and powerful. In the West men think that their own likes and dislikes of other men and things are guiding principles for them to act upon, even when they do not make of them the law of their lives and seek to impose them upon others.

Let those who complain that they have learned little in the Theosophical Society lay to heart the words written in an article in the *Path* for last February:— "The key in each degree is the *aspirant himself*". It is not "the fear of God" which is "the beginning of Wisdom", but the knowledge of SELF which is WISDOM ITSELF.

How grand and true appears, thus, to the student of Occultism who has commenced to realise some of the foregoing truths, the answer given by the Delphic Oracle to all who came seeking after Occult Wisdom — words repeated and enforced again and again by the wise Socrates: — MAN KNOW THYSELF.

[Chelaship has nothing *whatever* to do with means of subsistence or anything of the kind, for a man can isolate his mind entirely from his body and its surroundings. Chelaship is a *state of mind,* rather than a life according to hard and fast rules, on the physical plane. This applies especially to the earlier, probationary period, while the rules given in *Lucifer* for April [1889] last pertain properly to a later stage, that of actual occult training and the development of occult powers and insight. These rules indicate, however, the mode of life which ought to be followed by all aspirants *so far as practicable,* since it is the most helpful to them in their aspirations.

It should never be forgotten that Occultism is concerned with the *inner man*, who must be strengthened and freed from the dominion of the physical body and its surroundings, which must become his servants. Hence the *first* and chief necessity of Chelaship is a spirit of absolute unselfishness and devotion to Truth; then follow self-knowledge and self-mastery. There are all-important; while outward observance of fixed rules of life is a matter of secondary moment. - *Lucifer,* Volume 4 , June 1889, Page 348, note.]

SPIRITUALISM AND OCCULT TRUTH

The Spiritualist of Nov. 18th takes notice of the article published in *The Theosophist* for October under the heading "Fragments of Occult Truth," but it does not quite appreciate the objects with which that article was put forward, and still less the importance of its contents. To make further explanations intelligible to our own readers, however, we must first represent *The Spiritualist's* present remarks, which, under the heading of "Speculation-Spinning," are as follows:

> *The much-respected author of the best standard text-book on Chemistry in the English language, the late Prof. W. Allen Miller, in the course of a lecture at the Royal Institution, set forth certain facts, but expressed an objection to make known a speculative hypothesis which apparently explained the causes of the facts. He said that tempting but inadequately proved hypotheses, when once implanted in the mind, were most difficult to eradicate; they sometimes stood in the way of the discovery of truth, they often promoted experiments in a wrong direction, and were better out of the heads than in the heads of young students of science.*
>
> *The man who prosecutes original research must have some speculation in his head as he tries each new experiment. Such experiments are questions put to Nature, and her replies commonly dash to the ground one such speculation after another, but gradually guide the investigator into the true path, and reveal the previously unknown law, which can thenceforth be safely used in the service of mankind for all time.*
>
> *Very different is the method of procedure among some classes of psychologists. With them a tempting and plausible hypothesis enters the*

mind, but instead of considering it to be mischievous to propagate it as possessing authority before it is verified, it is thought clever to do so; the necessity for facts and proof is ignored, and it may be that a church or school of thought is set up, which people are requested to join in order that they may fight for the new dogma. Thus unproved speculations are forced upon the world with trumpet tongues by one class of people, instead of being tested, and, in most cases, nipped in the bud, according to the method of the man of science.

The religious periodicals of the day abound with articles consisting of nothing but speculations advanced by the authors as truths and as things to be upheld and fought over. Rarely is the modest statement made, "This may explain some points which are perplexing us, but until the verity of the hypothesis has been firmly demonstrated by facts, you must be careful not to let it rest in your mind as truth." By "facts" we do not necessarily mean physical facts, for there are demonstrable truths outside the realm of physics.

The foregoing ideas have often occurred to us while reading the pages of The Theosophist, *and have been revived by an interesting editorial article in the last number of that journal, in which the nature of the body and spirit of man is definitely mapped out in seven clauses. There is not one word of attempt at proof, and the assertions can only carry weight with those who derive their opinions from the authoritative allegations of others, instead of upon evidence which they have weighed and examined for themselves; and the remarkable point is that the writer shows no signs of consciousness that any evidence is necessary. Had the scientific method been adopted, certain facts or truths would have been made to precede each of the seven clauses, coupled with the claim that those truths demonstrated the assertions in the clauses, and negated all hypotheses at variance therewith.*

Endless speculation-spinning is a kind of mental dissipation, which does little good to the world or to the individuals who indulge therein, and has sometimes had in Europe a slight tendency to impart to the latter signs of Pharisaical self-consciousness of their being advanced religionists and philosophers, living in a diviner air than those who work to base their opinions on well-verified truths. If the speculators recognized their responsibility and imitated the example set them by the great and good Prof. Allen Miller, nine-tenths of their time would be set at liberty for doing good work in the world, the wasting of oceans of printing ink would be avoided, and mental energy which might be devoted to high uses would no longer run to waste. The minds of habitual dreamers and speculators may be compared to windmills incessantly at work grinding nothing.

Just at present there is far too much mental speculation afloat, and far too few people putting good ideas into practical form. Here in London, within the past year, grievous iniquities which might have been prevented, and grievous wrongs which might have been redressed, have abounded, and too few people have been at work ameliorating the sorrows and the sins immediately around them.

Now we do not want to discuss these questions with *The Spiritualist* in the way that rival religious sects might debate their differences. There can be no sectarianism in truth-seeking, and when we regard the spiritualists as seriously mistaken in many of the most important of the conclusions to which they have come, they must certainly be recognized as truth-seekers like ourselves. As a body, indeed, they are entitled to all possible honor for having boldly pursued their experiences to unpopular conclusions, caring more for what presented itself to them as the truth than for the good opinion of society at large. The world laughed at them for thinking their communications something beyond fraudulent tricks of impostors, for regarding the apparitions of their cabinets as visitors from another world. They knew quite well that the communications in a multitude of cases were no more frauds than they were baked potatoes, that people who called them such were talking utter folly, and in the same way that whatever the materialized "spirits" were, they were not in anything like all cases, even if they might be in some, the pillows and nightgowns of a medium's assistant. So they held on gallantly, and reaped a reward which more than compensated them for the silly success of ignorant outsiders, in the consciousness of being in contact with superhuman phenomena, and in the excitement of original exploration. Nothing that has ever been experienced in connection with such excitement by early navigators in unknown seas, can even have been comparable to the solemn interest which spiritual enquirers (*of the cultivated kind*) must have felt at first as they pushed off, in the frail canoe of mediumship, out into the ocean of the unknown world. And if they had realized all its perils one might almost applaud the courage with which they set sail, as warmly as their indifference to ridicule. But the heretics of one age sometimes become the orthodox of the next, and, so apt is human nature to repeat its mistakes, that the heirs of the martyrs may sometimes develop into the persecutors of a new generation. This is the direction in which modern spiritualism is tending, and that tendency, of all its characteristics, is the one we are chiefly concerned to protest against. The conclusions of spiritualism, inaccurate and premature as they are, are settling into the shape of orthodox dogma; while the facts of the great enquiry, numerous as they are, are still chaotic and confused, their collectors insist on working them up into specific doctrines about the future state, and they are often as intolerant of any dissent from these doctrines as the old-fashioned religionists were of them.

In fact, they have done the very thing which *The Spiritualist,* with an inaptitude born of complete misapprehension of what occult science really is, now accuses us of having done – they have given themselves wholly over to "speculation-spinning." It is fairly ludicrous to find this indictment laid at our door on account of our "Fragments." The argument of that paper was to the effect that spiritualists should not jump to conclusions, should not weave hasty theories, on the strength of *séance*-room experiments. Such and such appearances may present themselves; beware of misunderstanding them. You may see an apparition standing before you which you know to be perfectly genuine, that is to say, no trumpery imposture by a fraudulent medium, and it may wear the outward semblance of a departed friend, but do not on that account jump to the conclusion that it is the spirit of your departed friend, do not spin speculations from the filmy threads of any such delusive fabric. Listen first to the wisdom of the ancient philosophies in regard to such appearances, and permit us to point out the grounds on which we deny what seems to be the plain and natural inference from the facts. And then we proceeded to explain what we have reason to know is the accepted theory of profound students of the ancient philosophy. We were repeating doctrines as old as the pyramids, but *The Spiritualist*, not having hitherto paid attention to them, seems really to imagine that we have thrown them off on the spur of the moment as a hypothesis, as Figuier does with his conjectures in *The Day after Death*, or Jules Verne with his, in his *Voyage Round the Moon*. We cannot, it is true, quote any printed edition of the ancient philosophies, and refer the reader to chapter and verse, for an article on the seven principles; but assuredly all profound students of mystic literature will recognize the exposition on which we ventured, as supported, now in one way, now in another, by the cautiously obscure teaching of occult writers. Of course, the conditions of occult study are so peculiar that nothing is more difficult than to give one's "authorities" for any statement connected with it, but none the less is it really just as far from being "up in a balloon" as any study can be. It has been explained repeatedly that the continuity of occult knowledge amongst initiated adepts is the attribute about it which commends their explanations – absolutely to the acceptance of those who come to understand what initiation means, and what kind of people adepts are. From Swedenborg onwards there have been many seers who profess to gather their knowledge of other worlds from actual observation, but such persons are isolated, and subject to the delusions of isolation. Any intelligent man will have an intuitive perception of this, expressing itself in a reluctance on his part to surrender himself entirely to the assurances of any such clairvoyants. But in the case of regularly initiated seers it must be remembered that we are dealing with a long – an extraordinarily long – series of persons who, warned of the con fusing circumstances into which they pass when their spiritual perceptions are trained to range beyond material limits, are so enabled to penetrate to the actual realities of things, and who constitute a vast organized body of seers, who check each other's conclusions, test each other's discoveries and formulate their visions into a science of spirit as precise and entirely trustworthy as, in their humble way, are the conclusions, as far as they go, of any branch of physical science. Such initiates are in the position, as regards spiritual knowledge, that the regularly taught professor of a great university is in, as regards literary knowledge, and anyone can appreciate the superior claims of instruction which might be received from him, as compared with the crude and imperfect instruction which might be offered by the merely self- taught man. The initiate's speculations, in fact, are not spun at all; they are laid out before him by the accumulated wisdom of ages, and he has merely followed, verified and assimilated them.

But, it may be argued, if our statement about the teachings of this absolutely trustworthy occult science claims to be something more than assertion and hypothesis, it is an assertion, and, for the world at large, an hypothesis, that any such continuously-taught body of initiates is anywhere in existence. Now, in reference to this objection, there are two observations to be made. Firstly, that there is a large mass of writings to be consulted on the subject, and just as spiritualists say to the outer world, "if you read the literature of spiritualism, you will know how preposterous it is to continue denying or doubting the reality of spiritual phenomena," so we say to spiritualists, "if you will only read the literature of occultism it will be very strange if you still doubt that the continuity of initiation has been preserved." Secondly, we may point out that you may put the question about the existence of initiates altogether aside, and yet find in the philosophy of occultism, as expounded by those who do labor under the impression that they have received their teaching from competent instructors, such inherent claims to intellectual adoption, that it will be strange if you do not begin to respect it as an hypothesis. We do not say that the "Fragments" given in our October number constitute a sufficiently complete scheme *of* things to command conviction, in this way, on their own intrinsic merits, but we do say that even taken by themselves they do not offend intuitive criticism in the way that the alternative spiritual theory does. By degrees, as we are enabled to bring out more ore from the mine which yielded the "Fragments," it will be found that every fresh idea presented for consideration fits in with what has gone before, fortifies it, and is fortified by it in turn. Thus, is it not worth notice that even some notes we published in our December number in answer to enquiries about creation, help the mind to realize the way in which, and the materials with which, the elementaries in the one case, in the other the automatically acting Kâma Rûpa of the medium, may fashion the materialized apparition which the spiritualist takes for the spirit of his departed friend? It sometimes happens that a materialized spirit will leave behind as a memento of his visit some little piece cut from his spiritual (?) drapery. Does the spiritualist believe that the bit of muslin has come from the region of pure spirit from which the disembodied soul descends? Certainly no philosophically minded spiritualist would, but if as regards the drapery such a person would admit that this is fashioned from the cosmic matter of the universe by the will of the spirit which makes this manifest (accepting our theory so far), does it not rationally follow that all the "material" of the materialized visitor must probably be also so fashioned? And in that case, if the will of a spirit without form can produce the particular form which the sitter recognizes as his dead friend, does he not do this by copying the features required from some records to which, as a spirit, he has access; and, in that case again, is it not clear that some other spirit would equally have that power? Mere reflection, in fact, on the principles of creation will lead one straight to a comprehension of the utter worthlessness of resemblance in a materialized spirit, as a proof of identity.

Again, the facts of spiritual experience itself fortify the explanation we have given. Is it not the case that most spiritualists of long experience – omitting the few circumstanced in the very peculiar way that "M.A. Oxon." is, who are not in pursuit of dead friends at all – are always reduced sooner or later to a state of absolute intellectual exasperation by the unprogressive character of their researches. How is it that all these twenty years that spiritualists have been conversing with their departed friends their knowledge of the conditions of life in the next world is either as hazy still as the rambling imagination of a pulpit orator, or, if precise at all, grotesquely materialistic in its so-called spirituality? If the spirits were what the spiritualists think them, is it not obvious that they must have made the whole situation more intelligible than it is – for most people – whereas, if they are, what we affirm that they are really, is it not obvious that all they could do is exactly what they have done?

But, to conclude for the present, surely there need be no hostility, as some spiritual writers seem to have imagined, between the spiritualists and ourselves, merely because we bring for their consideration a new stock of ideas – new, indeed, only as far as their application to modern controversies is concerned, old enough as measured by the ages that have passed over the earth since they were evolved. A gardener is not hostile to roses because he prunes his bushes and proclaims the impropriety of letting bad shoots spring up from below the graft. With the spiritualists, students of occultism must always have bonds of sympathy which are unthought-of in the blatant world of earth-bound materialism and superstitious credulity. Let them give us a hearing; let them recognize us as brother-worshippers of truth, even though found in unexpected places. They cannot prove so oblivious of their own traditions as to refuse audience to any new plea, because it may disturb them in a faith they find comfortable. Surely it was not to be comfortable that they first refused to swim with the stream in matters of religious thought, and deserted the easy communion of respectable orthodoxy. Will spiritualism conquer incredulity only to find itself already degraded into a new church, sinking, so to speak, into armchairs in its second childhood, and no longer entitled to belief or vigorous enough for further progress? It is not a promising sign about a religious philosophy when it looks too comfortable, when it promises too indulgent an asylum for our speckled souls with houris of the Mohammedan Elysium, or the all too homelike society of the spiritualist's "Summer-land." We bring our friends and brethren in spiritualism no mere feather-headed fancies, no light-spun speculation, when we offer them some toil-won fragments of the mighty mountain of occult knowledge, at the base of whose hardly accessible heights we have learned to estimate their significance and appreciate their worth. Is it asked why we do not spread out the whole scroll of this much-vaunted philosophy for their inspection at once, and so exhibit clearly its all-sufficing coherence? That question at least will hardly be asked by thoughtful men who realize what an all-sufficient philosophy of the universe must be. As well might Columbus have been expected to bring back America in his ships to Spain. "Good friends, America will not come," he might have said, "but it is there across the waters, and if you voyage as I have done, and the waves do not smother you, mayhap you will find it too."

OCCULTISM VERSUS THE OCCULT ARTS

I oft have heard, but ne'er believed till now,
There are, who can by potent magic spells
Bend to their crooked purpose Nature's laws
   -Milton

In this month's "Correspondence" several letters testify to the strong impression produced on some minds by our last month's article, Practical Occultism. Such letters go far to prove and strengthen two logical conclusions.

(a) There are more well-educated and thoughtful men who believe in the existence of Occultism and Magic (the two differing vastly) than the modern materialist dreams of; and

(b) that most of the believers (comprising many Theosophists) have no definite idea of the nature of Occultism, and confuse it with the Occult sciences in general, the "Black art" included.

Their representations of the powers it confers upon man, and of the means to be used to acquire them, are as varied as they are fanciful. Some imagine that a master in the art, to show the way, is all that is needed to become a Zanoni. Others, that one has but to cross the Canal of Suez and go to India to bloom forth as a Roger Bacon or even a Count St. Germain. Many take for their ideal, Margrave with his ever-renewing youth, and care little for the soul as the price paid for it. Not a few, mistaking "Witch-of-Endorism", pure and simple, for Occultism — "through the yawning Earth from Stygian gloom, call up the meager ghosts to walks of light", and want, on the strength of this feat, to be regarded as full-blown Adepts. "Ceremonial Magic", according to the rules mockingly laid

37

down by Eliphas Levi, is another imagined *alter ego* of the philosophy of the Arhats of old. In short, the prisms through which Occultism appears, to those innocent of the philosophy, are as multicoloured and varied as human fancy can make them.

Will these candidates to Wisdom and Power feel very indignant if told the plain truth? It is not only useful, but it has now become *necessary* to disabuse most of them, and before it is too late. This truth may be said in a few words: There are not in the West half-a-dozen among the fervent hundreds who call themselves "Occultists" who have even an approximately correct idea of the nature of the science they seek to master. With a few exceptions, they are all on the highway to Sorcery. Let them restore some order in the chaos that reigns in their minds before they protest against this statement. Let them first learn the true relation in which the Occult Sciences stand to Occultism, and the difference between the two, and then feel wrathful if they still think themselves right. Meanwhile, let them learn that Occultism differs from Magic and other secret Sciences as the glorious sun does from a rush-light, as the immutable and immortal Spirit of Man — the reflection of the absolute, causeless and unknowable ALL — differs from the mortal clay — the human body.

In our highly civilised West, where modern languages have been formed, and words coined, in the wake of ideas and thoughts — as happened with every tongue, — the more the latter became materialised in the cold atmosphere of Western selfishness and its incessant chase after the goods of this world, the less was there any need felt for the production of new terms to express that which was tacitly regarded as absolute and exploded "superstition". Such words could answer only to ideas which a cultured man was scarcely supposed to harbour in his mind. "Magic", a synonym for jugglery;

"Sorcery", an equivalent for crass ignorance; and "Occultism", the sorry relic of crack-brained, mediaeval Fire-philosophers, of the Jacob Boehmes and the St. Martins are expressions believed more than amply sufficient to cover the whole field to "thimble-rigging". They are terms of contempt, and used generally only in reference to the dross and residues of the dark ages and its preceding aeons of paganism. Therefore have we no terms in the English tongue to define and shade the difference between such abnormal powers, or the sciences that lead to the acquisitions of them, with the nicety possible in the Eastern languages — pre-eminently the Sanskrit. What do the words "miracle" and "enchantment" (words identical in meaning after all, as both express the idea of producing wonderful things by *breaking the laws of nature*(!!) as explained by the accepted authorities) convey to the minds of those who hear, or who pronounce them? A Christian — breaking "of the laws of nature" notwithstanding — while believing firmly in the *miracles*, because said to have been produced by God through Moses, will either scout the enchantments performed by Pharaoh's magicians, or attribute them to the devil. It is the latter whom our pious enemies connect with Occultism, while their impious foes, the infidels, laugh at Moses, Magicians, and Occultists, and would blush to give one serious thought to such "superstitions". This, because there is no term in existence to show the difference; no words to express the lights and shadows, and draw the line of demarcation between the sublime and the true, the absurd and the ridiculous. The latter are the theological interpretations which teach the "breaking of the laws of Nature" by man, God, or devil; the former — the *scientific* "miracles" and enchantments of Moses and the Magicians *in accordance with natural laws*, both having been learned in all the Wisdom of the Sanctuaries, which were the "Royal Societies" of those days — and in true OCCULTISM. This last word is certainly misleading, translated as it stands, from the compound word *Gupta-*

Vidya, "Secret Knowledge". But the knowledge of what? Some of the Sanskrit terms may help us.

There are four (out of the many other) names of the various kinds of Esoteric Knowledge or Sciences given, even in the exoteric Puranas. There is

(1) *Yajna-Vidya* knowledge [The *Yajna*",says the Brahmans, "exists from eternity, for it proceeded forth from the Supreme One...in whom it lay dormant from ' *no* beginning.' It is the key to the TRAIVIDYA, the thrice sacred science contained in the Rig verses, which teaches the Yagus or sacrificial mysteries. 'The Yajna' exists as an invisible thing at all times; it is like the latent power of electricity in an electrifying machine, requiring only the operation of a suitable apparatus in order to be elicited. It is supposed to extend from the *Ahavaniya* or sacrificial fire to the heavens, forming a bridge or ladder by means of which the sacrificer can communicate with the world of gods and spirits, and even ascend when alive to their abodes". — Martin Haug's Aitareya Brahmana."This *Yajna* is again one of the forms of the Akasa; and the mystic word calling it unto existence and pronounced mentally by the initiated Priest is the *Lost Word* receiving impulse through WILL POWER"—"Isis Unveiled", Vol. I, Intr.. See *Aitareya Brahmana* by Haug.] of the occult powers awakened in nature by the performance of certain religious ceremonies and rites. (2) *Mahavidya*, the "great knowledge", the magic of the Kabalists and of the *Tantrika* worship, often Sorcery of the worst description. (3) *Guhya-Vidya*, knowledge of the mystic powers residing in Sound (Ether), hence in the Mantras (chanted prayers or incantations), and depending on the rhythm and melody used; in other words, a magical performance based on knowledge of the Forces of Nature and their correlation; and (4) ATMA-VIDYA,

a term which is translated simply "Knowledge of the Soul", *true Wisdom* by the Orientalists, but which means far more.

This is the only kind of Occultism that any Theosophist who admires "*Light on the Path*", and who would be wise and unselfish, ought to strive after. All the rest is some branch of the "Occult Sciences", *i.e.*, arts based on the knowledge of the ultimate essence of all things in the Kingdoms of Nature — such as minerals, plants and animals — hence of things pertaining to the realm of *material* Nature, however invisible that essence may be, and howsoever much it has hitherto eluded the grasp of Science. Alchemy, Astrology, Occult Physiology, Chiromancy, exist in Nature, and the *exact* Sciences — perhaps so called, because they are found in this age of paradoxical philosophies the reverse — have already discovered not a few of the secret of the above *arts*. But clairvoyance, symbolised in India as the "Eye of Siva", called in Japan, "Infinite Vision", is *not* Hypnotism, the illegitimate son of Mesmerism, and is not to be acquired by such arts. All the others may be mastered and results obtained, whether good, bad, or indifferent; but *Atma-Vidya* sets small value on them. It includes them all and may even use them occasionally, but it does so after purifying them of their dross, for beneficent purposes, and taking care to deprive them of every element of selfish motive. Let us explain: Any man or woman can set himself or herself to study one or all of the above specified "Occult Arts" without any great previous preparation, and even without adopting any too restraining mode of life. One could even dispense with any lofty standard of morality. In the last case, of course, ten to one the student would blossom into a very decent kind of sorcerer, and tumble down headlong into black magic. But what can this matter? The *Voodoos* and the *Dugpas* eat, drink, and are merry over hecatombs of victims of their infernal arts. And so do the amiable gentlemen vivisectionists and the *diploma-ed*

"Hypnotisers" of the Faculties of Medicine; the only difference between the two classes being that the Voodoos and Dugpas are *conscious*, and the Charcot- Richet crew *unconscious* Sorcerers. Thus, since both have to reap the fruits of their labours and achievements in the black art, the Western practitioners should not have the punishment and reputation without the profits and enjoyments they may get therefrom. For we say it again, *hypnotism* and *vivisection* as practiced in such Schools, are *Sorcery* pure and simple, *minus* a knowledge that the Voodoos and Dugpas enjoy, and which no Charcot-Richet can procure for himself in fifty years of hard study and experimental observation, Let, then, those who will dabble in magic, whether they understand its nature or not, but who find the rules imposed upon students too hard, and who, therefore, lay Atma- Vidya or Occultism aside — go without it. Let them become magicians by all means, even though they do become *Voodoos* and *Dugpas* for the next ten incarnations.

But the interest of our readers will probably center on those who are invincibly attracted towards the "Occult", yet who neither realise the true nature of what they aspire towards, nor have they become passion-proof, far less truly unselfish.

How about these unfortunates, we shall be asked, who are thus rent in twain by conflicting forces? For it has been said too often to need repetition, and the fact itself is patent to any observer, that when once the desire for Occultism has really awakened in a man's heart, there remains for him no hope of peace, no place of rest and comfort in all the world. He is driven out into the wild and desolate spaces of life by an ever-gnawing unrest he cannot quell. His heart is too full of passion and selfish desire to permit him to pass the Golden Gate; he cannot find rest or peace in ordinary life. Must he then inevitably fall into sorcery and black magic, and through many incarnations heap up for himself a terrible Karma? Is there no other road for him?

Indeed there is, we answer. Let him aspire to no higher than he feels able to accomplish. Let him not take a burden upon himself too heavy for him to carry. Without ever becoming a "Mahatma", a Buddha or a Great Saint, let him study the philosophy and the "Science of Soul", and he can become one of the modest benefactors of humanity, without any "superhuman" powers. *Siddhis* (or the Arhat powers) are only for those who are able to 'lead the life, to comply with the terrible sacrifices required for such a training, and to comply with them *to the very letter*. Let them know at once and remember always, that *true Occultism* or *Theosophy* is the "Great Renunciation of SELF", unconditionally and absolutely, in thought as in action. It is ALTRUISM, and it throws him who practises it out of calculation of the ranks of the living altogether. "Not for himself, but for the world, he lives", as soon as he has pledged himself to the work. Much is forgiven during the first years of probation. But no sooner is he "accepted' than his personality must disappear, and he has to become *a mere beneficent force in Nature*. There are two poles for him after that, two paths, and no midward place of rest. He has either to ascend laboriously, step by step, often through numerous incarnations and *no Devachanic break*, the golden ladder leading to Mahatmaship (the *Arhat* or *Bodhisattva* condition), or — he will let himself slide down the ladder at the first false step, and roll down into *Dugpaship*.

All this is either unknown or left out of sight altogether. Indeed, one who is able to follow the silent evolution of the preliminary aspirations of the candidates often finds strange ideas quietly taking possession of their minds. There are those whose reasoning powers have been so distorted by foreign influences that they imagine that animal passions can be so sublimated and elevated that their fury, force, and fire can, so to speak, be turned inwards; that they can be stored and shut up in one's breast, until their energy is, not expanded, but turned toward higher and more holy purposes: namely, *until their collective and unexpanded strength enables their possessor to enter the true Sanctuary of the Soul* and stand therein in the presence of the *Master* — the HIGHER SELF. For this purpose they will not struggle with their passions nor slay them. They will simply, by a strong effort of will, put down the fierce flames and keep them at bay within their natures, allowing the fire to smoulder under a thin layer of ashes. They submit joyfully to the torture of the Spartan boy who allowed the fox to devour his entrails rather than part with it. Oh, poor blind visionaries!

As well hope that a band of drunken chimney-sweeps, hot and greasy from their work, may be shut up in a Sanctuary hung with pure white linen, and that instead of soiling and turning it by their presence into a heap of dirty shreds, they will become masters in and of the sacred recess, and finally emerge from it as immaculate as that recess. Why not imagine that a dozen of skunks imprisoned in the pure atmosphere of a *Dgon-pa* (a monastery) can issue out of it impregnated with all the perfumes of the incenses used?... Strange aberration of the human mind. Can it be so? Let us argue.

The "Master" in the Sanctuary of our souls is "the Higher Self"— the divine spirit whose consciousness is based upon and derived solely (at any rate during the mortal life of the man in whom it is captive) from the Mind, which we have agreed to call the *Human Soul* (the "Spiritual Soul" being the vehicle of the Spirit). In its turn the former (the *personal* or human soul) is a compound, in its highest form, of spiritual aspirations, volitions, and divine love; and in its lower aspect, of animal desires and terrestrial passions imparted to it by its associations with its vehicle, the seat of all these. It thus stands as a link and a medium between the animal nature of man which its higher reason seeks to subdue, and his divine spiritual nature to which it gravitates, whenever it has the upper hand in its struggle with the *inner animal.* The latter is the instinctual "animal Soul", and is the hotbed of those passions which, as just shown, are lulled instead of being killed, and locked up in theirs breasts by some imprudent enthusiasts. Do they still hope to turn thereby the muddy stream of the animal sewer into the crystalline waters of life? And where, on what neutral ground, can they be imprisoned so as not to affect man? The fierce passions of love and lust are still alive, and they are allowed to still remain in the place of their birth — *that same animal soul;* for both the higher and the lower portions of the "Human Soul" or Mind reject such inmates, though they cannot avoid being tainted with them as neighbours. The "Higher Self" or Spirit is as unable to assimilate such feelings as water to get mixed with oil or unclean liquid tallow. It is thus the mind alone — the sole link and medium between the man of earth and the Higher Self — that is the only sufferer, and which is in incessant danger of being dragged down by those passions that may be reawakened at any moment, and perish in the abyss of matter. And how can it ever attune itself to the divine harmony of the highest Principle, when that harmony is destroyed by the mere presence, within the Sanctuary in preparation, of such animal passions? How can harmony prevail and conquer, when the soul is stained and distracted with the turmoil of passions and the terrestrial desire of the bodily senses, or even of the "Astral Man"?

For this "Astral" — the shadowy "double" (in the animal as in man) is not the companion of the *divine Ego* but of the *earthly body*. It is the link between the personal SELF, the lower consciousness of *Manas* and the Body, and is the vehicle of *transitory, not of immortal life*.

45

Like the shadow projected by man, it follows his movements and impulses slavishly and mechanically, and leans therefore to matter without ever ascending to Spirit. It is only when the power of the passions is dead altogether, and when they have been crushed and annihilated in the retort of an unflinching will; when not only all the lusts and longings of the flesh are dead, but also the recognition of the personal Self is killed out and the "Astral" has been reduced in consequence to a cipher, that the Union with the "Higher Self" can take place. Then when the "Astral" reflects only the conquered man, the still living but no more the longing, selfish personality, then the brilliant *Augoeides*, the divine SELF, can vibrate in conscious harmony with both the poles of the human Entity — the man of matter purified, and the ever pure Spiritual Soul — and stand in the presence of MASTER SELF, the Christos of the mystic Gnostic, blended, merged into, and one with IT for ever. [Those who would feel inclined to see three *Egos* in one man will show themselves unable to perceive the metaphysical meaning. Man is a trinity composed of Body, Soul, and Spirit; but *man* is nevertheless *one*, and is surely not his body. It is the latter which is the property, the transitory clothing of the man. The three "Egos" are MAN in his three aspects on the astral, intellectual or psychic, and the Spiritual planes, or states]

How, then, can it be thought possible for a man to enter the "straight gate" of occultism when his daily and hourly thoughts are bound up with worldly things, desires of possession and power, with lust, ambition, and duties which, however honourable, are still of the earth earthy? Even the love for wife and family — the purest as the most unselfish of human affections is a barrier to *real* occultism. For whether we take as an example the holy love of a mother for her child, or that of a husband for his wife, even in these feelings, when analyzed to the very bottom, and thoroughly sifted, there is still *selfishness* in the first, and an *égoisme à deux* in the second instance. What mother would not sacrifice without a moment's hesitation hundreds and thousands of lives for that of the child of her heart? and what lover or true husband would not break the happiness of every other man and woman around him to satisfy the desire of one whom he loves? This is but natural, we shall be told. Quite so, in the light of the code of human affections; less so, in that of divine universal love. For, while the heart is full of thoughts for a little group of *selves*, near and dear to us, how shall the rest of mankind fare in our souls? What percentage of love and care will there remain to bestow on the "great orphan"? And how shall the "still small voice" make itself heard in a soul entirely occupied with its own privileged tenants? What room is there left for the needs of Humanity *en bloc* to impress themselves upon, or even receive a speedy response? And yet, he who would profit by the wisdom of the universal mind, has to reach it through *the whole of Humanity* without distinction of race, complexion, religion, or social status. It is *altruism*, not *ego*-ism even in its most legal and noble conception, that can lead the unit to merge its little Self in the Universal Selves. It is to *these* needs and to this work that the true disciple of true Occultism has to devote himself if he would obtain *theo*-sophy, divine Wisdom and Knowledge.

The aspirant has to choose absolutely between the life of the world and the life of occultism. It is useless and vain to endeavour to unite the two, for no one can serve two masters and satisfy both. No one can serve his body and the higher Soul, and do his family duty and his universal duty, without depriving either one or the other of its rights; for he will either lend his ear to the "'still small voice" and fail to hear the cries of his little ones, or, he will listen but to the wants of the latter and remain deaf to the voice of Humanity. It would be a ceaseless, a maddening struggle for almost any married man, who would pursue *true* practical Occultism, instead of its *theoretical* philosophy. For he would find himself ever hesitating between the voice of the impersonal divine love of Humanity, and that of the personal, terrestrial love. And this could only lead him to fail in one or the other, or perhaps in both his duties. Worse than this. For, *whoever indulges, after having pledged himself to OCCULTISM,* in *the gratification of a terrestrial love or lust,* must feel an almost immediate result — that of being irresistibly dragged from the impersonal divine state down to the lower plane of matter. Sensual, or even mental, self-gratification involves the immediate loss of the powers of spiritual discernment; the voice of the MASTER can no longer be distinguished from that of one's passions, *or even that of a Dugpa*; the right from wrong; sound morality from mere casuistry. The Dead Sea fruit assumes the most glorious mystic appearance, only to turn to ashes on the lips, and to gall in the heart, resulting in:

Depth ever deepening, darkness darkening still;
Folly for wisdom, guilt for innocence;
Anguish for rapture, and for hope despair.

And once being mistaken and having acted on their mistakes, most men shrink from realizing their error, and thus descend deeper and deeper into the mire. And, although it is the intention that decides primarily whether *white or black magic* is exercised, yet the results even of involuntary, unconscious sorcery cannot fail to be productive of bad Karma. Enough has been said to show that *sorcery is any kind of evil influence exercised upon other persons, who suffer, or make other persons suffer, in consequence.*

Karma is a heavy stone splashed in the quiet waters of Life; and it must produce ever widening circles or ripples, carried wider and wider, almost *ad infinitum*. Such causes produced have to call forth effects and these are evidenced in the just laws of Retribution.

Much of this may be avoided if people will only abstain from rushing into practices neither the nature nor importance of which they understand. No one is expected to carry a burden beyond his strength and powers. There are "natural born magicians"; Mystics and Occultists by birth, and by right of direct inheritance from a series of incarnations and aeons of suffering and failures. These are passion-proof, so to say. No fires of earthly origin can fan into a flame any of their senses or desires; no human voice can find response in their souls, except the great cry of Humanity. These only may be certain of success. But they can be met only far and wide, and they pass through the narrow gates of Occultism because they carry no personal luggage of human transitory sentiments along with them. They have got rid of the feeling of the lower personality, paralyzed thereby the "astral" animal, and the golden, but narrow gate is thrown open before them. Not so with those who have to carry yet for several incarnations the burden of sins committed in previous lives, and even in their present existence. For such, unless they proceed with great caution, the golden gate of Wisdom may get transformed into the wide gate and the broad way "that leadeth unto destruction", and therefore "many be they that enter in thereby". This is the Gate of the Occult arts, practised for selfish motives and in the absence of the restraining and beneficent influence of ATMA-VIDYA. We are in the Kali Yuga and its fatal influence is a thousandfold more powerful in the West than it is in the East; hence the easy preys made by the Powers of the Age of Darkness in this cyclic struggle, and the many delusions under which the world is now labouring. One of these is the relative facility with which men fancy they can get at the "Gate" and cross the threshold of Occultism without any great sacrifice. It is the dream of most

Theosophists, one inspired by desire for Power and personal selfishness, and it is not such feelings that can ever lead them to the coveted goal. For, as well said by one believed to have sacrified himself for Humanity — "strait is the gate and narrow the way that leadeth unto life eternal", and therefore "few be they that find it".[Matt. viii, 14] So straight indeed, that at the bare mention of some of the preliminary difficulties the affrighted Western candidates turn back and retreat with a shudder....

Let them stop here and attempt no more in their great weakness. For, if while turning their backs on the narrow gate, they are dragged by their desire for the Occult one step in the direction of the broad and more inviting gates of that golden mystery which glitters in the light of illusion, woe to them! It can lead only to Dugpa-ship, and they will be sure to find themselves very soon landed on that *Via Fatale* of the *Inferno*, over whose portal Dante read the words:

Per me si va nella citta dolente
Per me si va nell' eterno dolore
Per me si va tra la perduta gente....

www.ingramcontent.com/pod-product-compliance
Lightning Source LLC
LaVergne TN
LVHW041501070426
835507LV00009B/729